ISBN-13: 9781700117465

Printed in the United States of America

This book is dedicated to all the people who have helped me learn and mature in the world of information security. Including the great infosec crowd at BSides Las Vegas, BSides Athens, BSides Cape Town, DEF CON, PasswordsCon and more.

This book is also dedicated to my family: Ingrid, Anthoula and Nick, for always supporting and putting up with me.

CONTENTS

FOREWORD

Baby-Doll dresses, The Rat Pack and Audio Cassettes. They all have something in common - they were made or became popular in the 60s. An era where human spaceflight was no longer science fiction, and touch tone telephones were becoming the norm. Something more was happening in the 60s however, especially towards the end of the decade. Computing power was growing. Data was becoming a "thing" and interconnected computers were evolving from theory to reality. Around the 1960's we entered an era that has come to be called "The Information Age". An age characterised by an increase in computing power, data, and overall control over information. In 1969 ARPA Net went online. The Advanced Research Projects Agency Network (ARPANET) was an early attempt to implement protocols that would eventually connect four US universities on a network. It would become the precursor to the Internet, a technology that has changed human lives and society on a global scale. You can read more about ARPANET here: https://en.wikipedia.org/wiki/ARPANET Everything in today's world is information. Your entire existence is a sum of digital information -such as your social security number, bank account, medical records and so on. With this movement of society into the Information Age, or Digital Age, a shift occurred in how criminals operate. Your gun-toting "baddies" who ran into banks to steal money have been superseded by cyber criminals who spend considerable digital resources on either hacking a bank, or attacking its clients. Guess who the client is? Yes, You! As humans, we have gone from a culture of paper, pen and physical queuing for services to one of electronic forms, websites and mobile phone applications. The problem is, the shift mentioned above has turned us into something else as well: Targets. Criminals with malicious intent have much easier access to target us via our emails and our connected devices. Cyber criminals can target any one of us. They do not need to come to us physically, or even know who we are. They just need to target us in the digital realm. This book does not aim to be a magic cure-all for your digital security. It does not contain cyber-se-

curity jargon and fancy words that technical people use. It will however give you practical guidance on how to secure yourself at home, at work, and your family. Although products and software can do a lot to protect us, they will always be limited by how much risk we introduce into our lives by our actions. Use the practical steps and information in this book to protect yourself, your family, and your workplace. Make notes, post-its or whatever you need to ensure you don't forget key tips and pertinent information (but please do not write your password on post-its!) The layout of this book includes theory, real stories and tables and diagrams to help you understand the concepts being explained. After each Chapter is a short review section. Each section gives you the key points from the chapter to take home with you and remember.

Dimitri Fousekis

Twitter: @rurapenthe0

DATA AND YOU

Your Life

I t's a cold winter morning in a small village in Switzerland. A businessman goes to a coffee shop to enjoy a nice hot cup of coffee and catch up on work. He takes his jacket off and hangs it on the chair as he sits down at the table. Looking outside, he sees the soft snow falling and settling on the street. He reaches for his mobile phone and checks the weather for the rest of the day. More snow, more cold. "You cannot deny the beauty and magic of the snow-covered streets and trees" he thinks to himself. He uses his cellphone to snap a picture of the view outside the window. Some fine wallpaper for his phone!

He takes out his laptop, turns it on and starts to get some work done. First up is to connect to the Wi-Fi, hopefully it's not going to be too slow today. Once online he logs into his e-mail. He watches closely as the counter begins to show the number of unread messages. Three…Six…Eleven. Today is going to be one of those days - so many e-mail messages to respond to and tasks to get done. He starts with the first message, leaning into that cup of coffee as the aroma makes him feel relaxed and ready to take on the world.

That could easily describe any one of us. Circumstances may change, and the way we interact with computers will differ, however a key point remains: We work with data every single day, every hour, almost every minute. A photo on the phone is data. The weather information is data. The Wi-Fi password is data. Data surrounds us, it defines a large portion of our lives. Did you lookup what you're going to watch on TV later - that's data. Are you going to send a text message to someone today? That's data. Around the world millions and millions of data are sent through corporate networks, the Internet, and other forms of connectivity.

Let's for a moment consider a person's life without data. If we had to strip every piece of electronic data about you, what would be left? Your social-security or equivalent information would be gone, therefore to any government entities you wouldn't exist. Your bank and financial information would be gone - no money for you. Your cell phone number and your details at your local phone company would not exist, therefore you would be uncontactable. You turn on the TV to watch something -

nope! No TV service for someone who does not exist and whose data is no longer in the customer system at your TV provider.

What about work? There's no work. No data means no access control to authorise your entry to the office. HR will have no idea who you are. You can't withdraw cash, you can't pay with any credit-cards and you can't order anything online because - no data. Seeing a trend here? Whether we want to admit it or not, we are the sum of our data about us. Relationships, friendships and emotional aspects aside, almost our entire existence in this world requires data about us. We don't exist without it. Therefore, we need to ask ourselves some very important questions: **What data exists about me? How important is that data? Would I be affected if any of that data was modified, lost or used by malicious persons?**

Understanding how data affects you is the first key to understanding how to secure yourself in a digital world. Think of all the data about you as being contained in a glass ball. You can handle that ball any way you want, you can put it down, and move it around. What happens, however, if you don't take care of that glass ball? It can break if not treated properly, leading to damaging consequences for your data. If you do not take care of your data you will run into some very serious risks. Common attacks that can happen when people don't secure their data include;
Theft of your personal information leading to identity theft or impersonation.
Access to your confidential files, accounts and transactions.
Ransomware infecting your computers.
Very bad people targeting your kids through the Internet.
Theft of your assets, money or other important material items.

If you are a high-profile individual, you should take even more precautions. Adversaries can use electronic means to steal your data and demand a very high ransom for it, or even threaten members of your family in cyberspace and demand a ransom to stop, or to not disclose some kind of confidential information about them or you.

Data exists in many states. Each state will determine how it should be secured. When you edit a document on your computer, and you save it - **that is data at rest.** Keep in mind that data at rest can also include anything you have backed-up or archived to other storage devices like USB memory, CD/DVD discs and so on. At a company, data at rest could also include data backed-up to magnetic tape, long-term storage disks and so on.

The risk with data at rest is that it is waiting for access. If you do not properly control who or what has access to it, you increase your chances of losing confidential data. For example, consider our businessman at the coffee shop we mentioned earlier. He pulls out a USB memory device (or "stick") and copies some files from it to his laptop. He unplugs the device and then leaves it on the table behind his empty cup of coffee. When it's time to go, he is in a rush and gets up quickly to leave - forgetting the USB device on the table.

He has lost data at rest. Anybody who picks up the device can get his data from it (if you're thinking "why did he not encrypt it?" you've jumped ahead a few chapters. We'll get to that).

The fact is most of us copy data to these types of removable devices and we do not give second thought as to what will happen if the device is stolen or misplaced.

Now, imagine that you are e-mailing that document on your computer to a friend or family member. Your **data is now in motion**. This is also known a data in transit. It refers to data that is moving between electronic systems and networks. As soon as that data arrives at the target recipient's mailbox it is at rest. First on their e-mail server and then on their computer when they save it. At any given moment there are millions if not billions of data in transit around the world. Data is split up into "packets" when it is transmitted across networks. Think of data in transit as mail going through a post-office. Every envelope is a "piece" of data. Thousands of envelopes are moving through a post-office at every moment. Some are being routed here, others are routed there.

Now comes the risk. Imagine if someone with malicious intent starts opening and reading the envelopes. They open each one, see what it says, re-seal the envelope and send it on its way. The person receiving the envelope has no idea that it has been viewed by someone else. Yet over a period of time, this malicious person could read hundreds or thousands of letters and the confidential information in them.

The risk for data in transit on electronic networks is the same. Such data is open to attacks by malicious persons who want to intercept the data.

The third state of data involves **data in use**. This does not particularly mean data that you, as a human, are using yourself. It refers to data in use on an electronic system. For example, the document you are editing on your computer is in use by the computer as it is being temporarily stored in the CPU (Central Processing Unit, I.e. the main number cruncher of the computer), or in RAM (Random Access Memory - the temporary storage memory of a computer). In this state, the data is vulnerable to various attacks such as corruption of data, other programs using the data without permission and modifying of the data without your permission.

To recap, the three states of data are **data at rest, data in motion/transit and data in use.** Since data is such an important, integral part of our lives, almost all the information in this book will relate to data that is in one of these states. It is important to remember that no matter what cyber-attack occurs it involves data, and it involves data in one of those states. If we did not have data, there would be nothing for someone to act maliciously against. Even if someone wants to negatively impact YOU, they are affecting data. Of course, we're excluding physical attacks since in that case they are actually harming you - not your data.

The diagram below shows the relationship between your data and you. Notice how data revolves around our lives and our existence. As mentioned earlier, without data in the age we live in, we simply would not be able to function.

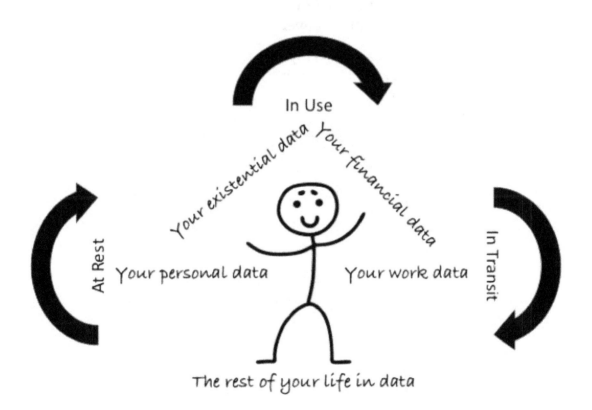

The risks that cyber security attacks can pose to you will affect many different kinds of data and the state of that data. When you are infected by ransomware for example, that can affect data at rest, and such data can include your documents, financial data, existential data such as photos of yourself and your family, and much more.

Let's recap this chapter as it forms a basis for this entire book. I've put the main points down in bullet form to make it easier for you to remember and/or make notes of your own;

All information that is stored electronically is data. Data surrounds us in our everyday lives from our mobile phones, to information about us, our finances, lives (existential) and so on.

Without data we cannot work, live in society or manage our lives and finances. It has direct impact on our families as well.

Pieces of data can be in any one of three possible states: At rest, in motion/transit or in use. We have to make sure we secure our data in any of those three states. However, data at rest and in use are more under our control that data in motion. We can apply good practices to secure them all, however.

As you continue reading this book, my aim is for you to understand how to make simple, yet affective decisions on managing the security of your data. This includes actions you can take to better secure your data and what to do if you find you have been hacked or some form of electronic attack takes place against you.

In the cyber security industry, professionals refer to what is known as the "CIA triad". Not to be confused with the spy agency that pounces on you in black SUV's, the CIA Triad refers to a triangle who's three points have the three most important aspects of cyber security - Confidentiality, Integrity and Availability. Together they abbreviate as CIA. Yes, they could also be AIC, IAC and so forth but come on - CIA sounds so much better!

Although we are not going into deep technical discussion about security in this book - that is not its purpose, I mentioned the CIA Triad because it forms a basis for all the points and practical information contained herein. Your data always needs to remain Confidential, to maintain its Integrity (I.e. not change without your permission) and to be Available. For example, a Ransomware attack affects the Integrity and Availability of your data by encrypting its contents and preventing you from being able to work with the said data.

Also, the reason we use a triangle in the CIA Triad is because a triangle cannot exist if you remove one of its sides. Holistic security of your data and systems also cannot be complete if you do not address all three aspects of the CIA Triad.

Time to move on. We're going to now discuss cyber security and your workplace or employment. You may be surprised by what the next chapter says about you and your workplace when it comes to security.

Your Work

Remember the businessman we spoke about earlier? He finishes up at the coffee shop and goes into the office to work for the day. He gets some more coffee, adjusts his seat at his desk to be comfortable and logs onto the corporate network.

How much value do you place on your workplace security? I've included a small quiz below for you to take, and we will analyse the answers. Answer it honestly and then proceed to the next part to analyse the reason for the questions and the possible responses and what they mean.

Workplace Quiz

I use the same password at work as I do for my home computer or personal email account - Yes or No?

My personal information is very important to me. My personal email account, Facebook and other social networking passwords are much longer than my work network or email password - Yes or No?

If something happens to my work computer and a hacker/malicious person can access the company data, the blame falls entirely on the company for not securing my computer properly. Yes or No?

I often have workmates who forget their passwords, so I just give them my details to use at work as it is easier than waiting forever for someone to reset their password. Yes or No?

The purpose of the quiz above is to ascertain one simple fact: Do you place equal value on your workplace data as you do on your personal data? Is it of equal importance to you that a hacker could read your work email vs your personal email? If a hacker compromised your Facebook account, would it be a bigger or smaller problem for you than a hacker compromising an application you use at work?

There is an unfortunate trait that humans have towards protecting what is personally theirs a lot more than protecting what is not theirs. The data at a company belongs to the company. The company is rich, it has money and, let us face it, has little interest in your personal life. However, should this be the case? Should you have containers of higher and lower security in your mind where you allocate personal items and where you allocate work items? The short answer is: No. Of course, things are never simple so let us analyse why that is the case.

If you answered yes for Question 1 above, this is not necessarily a bad thing. It means you're using a password across multiple systems (more on that later), but importantly it means you are not downgrading the security of one partition of data over another. Your password for both your personal and work email accounts could be the same - and it could be a very strong and secure password. The key comes in however if you answered "No". This is because the next question I'll ask you is Question 2 on the list: Do you have a longer, more difficult password for work email and applications or for personal email, Facebook and so forth? You may be surprised at how you answer that because it could give away what we have been talking about all this time. You place more value in your personal data and thus have a better personal data password than you do for your workplace data.

Now, some may argue that your work password is weaker/shorter/simpler because you use it all the time at work and it is inconvenient to have to keep re-entering it all the time. We are not here to discuss usage semantics, however, a key point to keep in mind is that very often, ease-of-use and minimal effort do not align well with security best-practises. Yes, a password of "1234" is easy to use and repeat many times throughout the day. It is also easy for an attacker to guess with minimal expertise or even time. In fact, "1234" is so weak, if you are using it now, I recommend putting this book down and changing it. Change it! Back? Good, let's continue...

Questions 1 and 2 ascertained whether or not we place equal importance on the security of data between our personal lives and our work lives. Now let's examine your answer to Question 3;

Question 3 and 4 highlight another important point in the workplace: Responsibility. Do I feel responsible for my behaviour in the workplace to the extent that I understand that my decisions regarding security matters could affect the whole company? A company is responsible for ensuring there are policies and procedures in place for Cyber Security. This includes passwords, what kind of data should or should not be encrypted, use of hardware and any applicable websites or web applications within the company. How do I view this policy? Do I know what the person I've shared my password with is doing with it? Are they looking after the data I'm responsible for? Can I trust them to do so?

In general, company policies tend to be shelved in a file or electronic document and little emphasis gets placed on the content until something goes terribly wrong. Suddenly all the policies and procedures are brought out and laid bare to find who dared to break those policies and a witch-hunt ensues.

This is a critical understanding we need to have about corporate security in the workplace. You may be just an employee, but your actions with regards to cyber security (or lack thereof) will have financial impact on the company. That impact will affect you in some way. It will affect your colleagues in some way. In extreme cases it could affect the entire company to the extent that it cannot function. If you were the reason your company was breached and lost millions of dollars through data theft, compliance fines and other problems - would you really be wanting to have a discussion about whether or not the blame should be 100% yours or the company's? That situation is best avoided altogether.

Corporates are responsible for ensuring their policies are properly implemented, aligned to best-practice and reasonable enough for staff to actually adhere to them. I once saw a company whose password policy was: Minimum 16 characters, At least two digits, must have lower and upper case and at least 3 special characters. The result? Walking through their offices, one was bombarded by yellow Post-It notes stuck over staff monitors with their password written down so that they could actually remember it. Then, the company enforced password changes every 20 days. That's just suicide for password security because the amount of people writing down passwords or forgetting them and having to call the help-desk - will far outweigh any benefit to using such strong passwords.

As a staff member, as an individual, you are responsible for keeping your data safe at the workplace as much as you are in your personal life. We've all heard of the horror stories of companies losing millions or even billions to breaches cause by security flaws. Almost all those security flaws were due to a person, or persons, who failed to implement one or more secure practices with regards to data. Whether your job is to type up letters for the CEO, or you are an administrator for thousands of servers - you own the data you are responsible for. You must secure it accordingly. You should treat it as though it's made of glass. Protect it as though it is your personal data. Your attitude towards security is like an umbrella, underneath it is your personal and work data. Treat them equally and secure them properly and you can only benefit yourself and the company that pays your salary. Create holes in the umbrella and you're going to be sitting with a lot of leaks...

YOUR ATTITUDE TOWARDS SECURITY IS LIKE AN UMBRELLA
THE SECURITY UMBRELLA PROTECTS YOUR DATA BELOW IT
THE MORE YOU CLOSE THE UMBRELLA, THE MORE YOU ARE EXPOSED

We've spent some time discussing what data is all about. Hopefully from this chapter you have begun to understand how important data is. It forms the integral part of everything this book is about. It also forms an integral part of everything your life is about. In the following chapters we are going to dig into the practical aspects of Cyber Security and what you can do to make yourself more secure.

Your Take-Away for Chapter 1

- Data affects all of us. We cannot exist today without data.
- You need to understand how theft of your data, modification of your data or loss of your data can affect your life.
- You should have the same attitude towards protecting your data at work, as you do for your personal data. In the end, it all affects you in some way or another.
- Your data spans multiple domains of your life including your personal information, work information, your photographs, information about you and your family and much more.

PHISHING, SMISHING AND VISHING

Got Bait?

G rowing up, my family used to often go on fishing trips to the South Coast of South Africa. About 120KM (74 miles) South of Durban is a fishing resort that is right on the beach. From your chalet you could literally cast your fishing rod into the ocean. Of course, for better casting distance one would walk onto the beach sand, outside the chalet entrance.

I remember early mornings around 4:30am, darkness all around and just the moonlight reflecting off the waves. You would take your fishing rod, put on the hooks and bait and cast into the water. The fish would bite almost instantly, causing much excitement as you felt the rod pull in short, distinct bursts, as the fish were hooked.

The reason I'm mentioning that, apart from a little bit of nostalgia - is that it is what the malicious cyber security action of Phishing is based on. The similarities are extremely close and so we'll use fishing, as in the normal catch-a-fish-to-eat kind, to explain how attackers perform Phishing attacks. Then we will cover how to protect ourselves against such attacks.

When you go fishing, you have a few things you need to arrange and plan for. We can sum-up what is required to be a successful fisherman in three points:

A fishing rod, to get your bait and hook into the ocean as well as a reel and line to bring back in what you catch.

A hook, best chosen to properly catch the fish you are fishing for. Sometimes it includes other additions like a sinker, and/or float to make it more effective and;

Bait. Probably the most important aspect here because, unless you're fishing with dynamite, you actually need something a fish wants to eat if you want to hook and catch it.

In choosing the above three items for your fishing trip, you would spend time analysing the area you are going to, the type of fish that are in the water and when it is the best time to fish. Additionally, you may choose to swap out bait for a lure - a "fake" bait and hook combination. Either way, it does a similar job to what a normal bait and a hook do: Lure the fish, get them to bite, and hook them.

Let's now compare the above analogy to a phishing attack. A phishing attack is when someone tries to obtain confidential or sensitive information about you, such as your credit-card details, username and passwords, social security (ID) numbers and so forth - for malicious intent and disguised as a trustworthy entity.

Remember, when we go fishing - we don't just dangle a hook and hope fish will catch themselves. The bait hides the hook under the guise of food, or we could say: a trustworthy entity. In a Phishing attack the malicious person wants to either get information from you that they should not have, or they want to actually steal from you and need information to do it. Their aim could be to steal money, issue transactions on your credit cards, access your internet banking or steal-and-sell your identity. Let us now examine how the malicious parties go about their phishing attack.

The Phishing Rod

In order to extend their hook and bait out into the wild, the attacker needs a method of transporting it out onto the Internet. In this case, much like a fishing rod gives a fisherman the ability to swing it and cast their bait and hook a great distance, so too the *phisherman* uses mediums such as E-mail, Social Media, Websites and advertising on the Internet to get their bait out there. The most common method is bulk e-mails. The more they can send, the more potential there is to catch something. Remember, a fisherman doesn't cast his bait into a tiny little rock pool and hope to catch a big fish. He aims for the wide-open water. So too, malicious *phishermen* want to get as much mileage out of their fake email as they can, so they aim far and wide.

Always be on the lookout for emails, messages through social media, and other forms of contact that try to obtain information from you. In this day and age, it is extremely rare to have somebody from a legitimate financial institution phone you and ask for your details. They should also never email you and ask for details either. Any exceptions to this should be met with extreme caution.

The Phishing Hook

Once that e-mail has gone out to multiple parties. It needs to accomplish something. It needs to be designed to allow you to interact with it. Either by providing a link to a website, or a number to call or simply to reply to that email message (albeit replies are usually rare, as the majority of phishing emails come from invalid addresses or compromised accounts).

When you respond to the phishing message - that is when you are hooked. There is still some time to break free however, but as you provide more and more information or are taken deeper into the storyline that is trying to obtain information from you, you are making that hook sink in deeper and deeper.

The Phishing Bait

The bait is where it's at. You can run a fishing rod and hook around all day but with nothing to attract the fish to it - your chances of catching anything are minimal at best. The bait is there to lure the fish towards the hook, finally biting and getting trapped. It ties everything together into a successful fish or *phish*.

Bait in phishing attacks works the same way. Some kind of elaborate story or call to action is presented to you, and you are almost obliged (it's still your choice) to reply and give the information needed. Sometimes the bait is masked - inside other bait. Allowing you to "nibble" pieces off and think that there is no hook here so it must be safe. Until you get comfortable and take a bigger bite...

Phishing attacks rely on a few social engineering techniques. Although we cover social engineering later on, we need to discuss some of it now as it pertains to phishing. Social engineering is when you use deception of various forms (often electronic) to manipulate someone into divulging sensitive information or performing an action they otherwise would not do. Social engineering plays on many psychological aspects of the human mind.

One such aspect, which phishing attacks rely on - is greed. Greed is a part of human nature and whether we want to admit or not, we all have a measure of it in us. Marketing adverts at stores play on that aspect of social engineering. For example, the age old: "Only 5 items left at this price!" or "Today only!" plays on our greed to have something someone else may not, and also the use of a deadline forces us to react faster than we can think. Further, *scarcity* is used. It refers to making something you don't need sound so scarce that you have to have it. "Do I need another Microwave?" is not as common a thought as "There's only 5 Microwaves left at this price; I won't get another like it! I should buy it!".

Phishing attacks do the same. I'm sure you've seen many examples that revolve around the following wording:

"Dear Sir/Mam, the United Nations have approved a trust fund worth $10 000 000 US to be made available to 3 random individuals as part of their gift campaign. Only THREE (3) people can benefit from this. Will you be one of them? Send us your details now so that we can add you to the selection campaign. Ignoring this email could cost you millions of dollars! This offer closes in 24 hours!"

Granted, the first thing that should stand out in the above message is the lack of grammatical and spelling errors I did not include. Nonetheless, messages along similar lines to this one go out all the time in various forms.

Analysing the above message, can you see the social engineering at play?

"United Nations" - plays on authority. We tend to be interested in a message coming from an authoritative source.

"$10 000 000" - plays on greed. Who wouldn't like a share of that kind of money!

"Only THREE (3)" - note the use of *scarcity* here. It's something rare, hard to come by, and so you need to fight for it to be one of those lucky people and not one of the losing parties.

"Will you be one of them?" - creates a feeling of "I don't want to NOT be one of them.."

"Ignoring this email..." - Almost a threat as it were, but one that subtly makes us think, it doesn't put us on the defensive.

"This offer closes in 24 hours!" – Rush-rush. To make sure you have little time for logic to play its part.

Did you notice the call to action, buried in between everything else? *"Send us your details.."* This sentence is not heavily written in bold, nor repeated for emphasis. This is because once we are socially engineered properly and we take the bait - the action (getting hooked) is easily assimilated by our minds to be carried out.

We live in a time where data breaches and "leaks" of our personal information are everywhere. Therefore, do not assume that it is impossible for someone to have your email address, or even your physical address. Unfortunately, data breaches are far and wide and some we do not even know about. This means it is always possible to receive a phishing attack to our email address and it may even have some valid information about us.

At the end of the day, Data is what is being stolen from you in a phishing attack. That data could lead to financial or other losses as well, but at the core, it's data. Protecting our data, like we discussed in Chapter 1, is key to protecting against phishing attacks. Let's spend some time now considering how we can defend ourselves against a phishing attack.

A phishing attack is when someone tries to obtain confidential or sensitive information about you, such as your credit-card details, username and passwords, social security (ID) numbers and so forth - for malicious intent and disguised as a trustworthy entity. Usually the message is sent to you via email.

A smishing attack is when someone tries to obtain the above information using

SMS or other mobile messaging services to send you a crafted message that requires you to either click a link or reply with information.

A vishing attack is when someone tries to obtain the above information using a voice call - and pretending to be your bank, or other important party.

Swimming in Dangerous Waters

Could a fish avoid being caught by a fisherman and his fishing equipment? In actual fact, fish often do get away from a fisherman. They are very sensitive to the wrong movement, certain colours and of course their food (read bait) moving in an unnatural way. For the most part, fish do get caught. Also, many don't. Unfortunately, the same rule applies for many people around the world when it comes to phishing attacks.

By now, malicious experts know some tricks of the trade that can make phishing even more successful. Targeting older, or younger people is often lucrative because they may be more trusting of other humans and messages they see. Using hacked email credentials to send their phishing attacks from legitimate sounding addresses, and hosting their phishing websites on compromised servers that would not be flagged for being known for malicious activity.

Can we defend against phishing? Most certainly we can. Below is a list, in order of how defence against phishing should occur. Note that this order is not cast in stone, but I am making a point regarding us as humans not relying so much on technology to catch these for us:

Human recognition of an e-mail or message that is malicious and is deemed phishing.

Automated (heuristic) software detecting e-mails or messages that are deemed phishing.

Browser-plugins and other systems that alert us when giving our details to unsecured, suspicious or known malicious websites.

The reason human recognition of phishing attacks is No 1 on the defensive list, is, in my opinion, that our minds are perfectly geared towards identifying these malicious cases. It sounds ironic, since our minds can also be socially engineered - however our thought process combined with logic can far outperform any machine trying to do the same.

When you get an e-mail, advert, social media message and so forth - ask yourself some key questions;

Does this originate from somebody I know? If it does, does it sound like something they would usually send me, or does it not have their style of writing and word choice?

Does the message contain repetitive urgency and words that make it sound like I have to act now or I'm going to miss out on something? Check for *scarcity.*

Is it asking for my details? (Any kind) or is it asking me to contact someone to provide them with details? Would a reputable company do that?

Is it asking for information that corporate institutions **never** should ask for: My password, my username or PIN?

Is it promising a large reward for very little effort - such as just giving some information?

Has another Prince/King/Queen died?

Does this just generally give me an uneasy feeling?

Point 7 should not be ignored. Our intuition can often spot something we may not be fully aware of and that feeling at the back of our minds that something could be wrong - could be right. Of course, one does not want to become suspicious of everything, but if you answered "Yes" to at least two questions above, you could be treading in dangerous water if you continue interacting.

What if you are still unsure? If the message appears to be from a corporate or some kind of identifiable entity - contact them **by looking up their details separately** and ask if they did send that email out. In many cases, and especially with financial institutions, they like to know if phishing e-mails or messages go out that affect them, and they have dedicated e-mail addresses where one can forward such information to. Remember, don't contact them by replying to the potentially malicious e-mail. Attackers know someone might do this and could have an elaborate, but basic, call centre setup to handle your calls and phish information from you while pretending to be the party on the other side.

Coming to the tools that are out there to help us, we will touch on the wide variety of Internet Security and Cyber Security protection suites available. These days, almost all email systems whether corporate or "free", have some kind of spam and phishing email protection built in. For the ones that do get through, there are products such as Kaspersky Internet Security, AVG Internet Security, F-Secure Internet Security and so forth. I am not going to recommend one over the other as the purpose of this book is to educate you without promoting any products. My suggestion is to research them all, check out reviews and find what is cost-effective and works well for you.

These tools work by using pattern recognition, machine learning (heuristics) and large databases of known malicious e-mail or message sources to protect you by marking or classifying these messages when they enter your device. The tools should act as a backup for you, not be a finite assessment of all messages. Just because your protection software failed to mark something as phishing-related does not mean it cannot be malicious. Equally, just because it marked something as phishing - does not always mean it is. This is why it is so important to have the human factor in this equation and not rely solely on what your e-mail client or other system tells you.

Sometimes the goal of a phishing attack is not to have you supply information, but rather to infect your system with some or other kind of malware. It could be a file that you are asked to run, or something embedded into the message in the hopes that a vulnerable system would run it and be compromised. It should go without saying that if an email looks suspicious you would also never want to click on any attachments. Some email clients also warn you that content could be dangerous - it is a good idea to adhere to such information.

Spear Phishing

Let us go back to our actual fishing scenario again. In some cases, a fisherman chooses not to use a fishing rod, but to rather use a spear-gun or a hand-held spear and hunt specific fish. In this case rather than casting bait out and waiting for a fish to bite, a spear fisherman targets a specific fish, lines-up the spear tip and fires at the fish.

The same principle applies to Spear Phishing. Unlike the broad targeting of phishing attacks, a spear phishing attack is targeted to an individual or group of individuals. There is method and thought put into the target (you) to customise the attack and make it more lucrative and thus more successful. In many cases a spear-phishing attack runs on the back of a phishing attack. Having received more information about general targets, the attacker would switch to a spear-phishing attack with specific information and victims in mind.

We generally get less suspicious of an email or message that has some kind of personal information about us. For example, an email sent to: "The Homeowner" may make us be suspicious about the content. Whereas an email sent to "Jane Goodall[1]" sounds more personal and if that is your name, you may be less inclined to be suspicious. Don't! The whole purpose of spear phishing is to let your guard down by targeting the attack using specific information obtained through other channels. The same principles apply in a spear phishing attack as they do in a normal phishing attack. Once you look past the personalised information, the attack is the same and the end goal is the same.

Smishing

Although the process of phishing information from someone generally follows the same process, the method used can change. In a Smishing attack, the phishing is done via SMS or Text Message instead of email. The modus operandi remains the same as normal phishing. The messages usually pretend to be from your bank or other trusted source and due to the limited space in an SMS message, it tends to get to the point quickly to move you to action. For example, by telling you that your bank account has been locked-out, or that some important services will be cancelled if you don't act quickly. The message then contains a web link for you to follow (which you would never do).

Vishing

You probably have worked out what this is from its name. Vishing is the method of phishing using Voice Calls. Vishing can be especially dangerous because its a real-time attack and in some cases the attackers could be ready to perform some form of banking transaction or login to an important site, and are just waiting for information from you. Never respond to voice calls asking for your credit-card number to prevent fraud, or to request any OTP (One-Time-Pin) sent to your device. Further if you use an application to approve transactions, never approve such based on a phone call you received. If in doubt, always hang up and contact the Bank or Call Center of the system you are using with the phone number you have on hand for them.

In Summary

Phishing attacks are common and due to their continued success, we will see more and more of them. Further, with the advancements in technology, leaked data on the internet to use as sources of data as well as emerging techniques, phishing will continue to be an avenue used by many attackers to complete their goal.

The upside is that defending against such attacks is also becoming more and more effective. Technology is always advancing in order to detect attacks, and - the fact that you're reading this book - knowledge of the problem is making it easier for people to identify these risks and thus making it harder for attackers to be successful.

Here is a chart you can use to identify if an email is phishing or not. There is no perfect method but if you combine it with sensibility and human intuition it will work well for you;

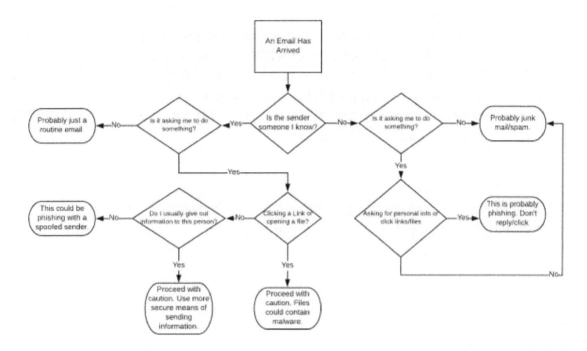

In the end, Phishing attacks are like all other criminal enterprises; Their success rate depends on how well the target (read: you) is protected, knowledgeable, and able to actively defend against it. What you will notice in this book is that it all comes down to maintaining a balance between suspicion and efficiency. You should not get to a point where you assume all emails are unsafe and never reply to anyone ever again. Neither should you assume everyone out there is your friend or that technology is always going to protect you. A good balance results in a secure outcome.

Phishing can be used as a platform not only to get information from you, but to try and get you to run infected programs with viruses and/or malware. Our next chapter covers this aspect of securing yourself...

Your Take-Away for Chapter 2

- Phishing is a real and ongoing attack method used by criminals to get personal information from you or to obtain banking details, credit-card numbers, etc.
- A Phishing attack is made up of multiple phases, and you should be able to identify and protect yourself at any of the stages.
- Read emails carefully. Do not reply to everyone asking you for information and if it looks suspicious, rather ignore it.
- Smishing and Vishing are alternative forms of Phishing using SMS or Text Messages and Voice Calls.

---

[1] The names portrayed in this production are fictitious. No identification with actual persons (living or deceased), places, buildings, and products is intended or should be inferred

BANKING AND FINANCE

Protect Your Banking

A common target for criminals is your bank account. It provides a quick and often easy method for obtaining financial gain. As we benefit from more and more products designed to make our lives easier, so too do criminals have more means to attack these products. We will cover some of the common areas where you will be at risk, not only electronically but also physically when it comes to your banking.

Credit Cards And Bank Cards

Bank cards are as common to all of us as cash. They were first used around 1967 as a secure and alternative means to carrying cash, and to facilitate payments anywhere in the world. They are almost impossible to live without, even in lands where cash is still a primary method of payment. Unfortunately, as the use of bank cards increased, so did the fraud being committed on them. Even with the advent of contactless bank cards (they use a microchip and transmitter to allow you to "tap" a payment device instead of swiping or inserting the card) people still experience theft occurring on their bank accounts. To protect yourself from card fraud, keep the following important points in mind;

Never give out information about your account such as your full name, contact numbers or bank account numbers to persons you don't know, websites you don't trust or forms you cannot account for. Even such minimal information without passwords and card number can put you at risk.

When making payments online, ensure that you only provide your card details to reputable websites. (See What About SSL? Do I need a VPN? In Chapter 6)

Never type your card details into insecure online forms such as customer service or tickets for assistance.

Don't put card details into email messages.

Activate your card or bank's secure payments system for online transactions such as Verified by Visa or 3DSecure. These require you to provide an additional verification step for online transactions with your card. (Some merchants can override this, but then the risk of fraud becomes the merchant's, not yours)

Ensure no one watches you entering your PIN either at ATM machines or POS devices.

There should be no reason anymore for a person to walk away with your card to process payment, as payment machines are now wireless. Avoid letting your card out of sight.

Although not easy to clone the chip on "tap-to-pay" cards, avoid leaving your bank card lying around where it could be cloned wirelessly (or physically via the chip).

Although we use our bank cards every day, and banks have a lot of security processes in place to protect cards, we need to take precautions to ensure they are not compromised.

Internet Banking, Mobile Banking and App Banking

Internet Banking - via mobile app or a web-browser, is still a lucrative target for attackers. The reason being, once such system is compromised, it can result in immediate funds transfer through electronic payments. There are many controls in place currently to protect one from fraud via Internet Banking and Mobile Banking. They include;

The requirement for multi-factor login or confirmation of transactions via a One-Time-Pin App, SMS or token device.

Checks by Mobile Apps on whether your phone SIM card was changed and/or swapped.

Confirmation of all transactions performed via Email, SMS or App notifications so you can be aware of any activity on your account.

App verification via your phone's biometric services like FaceID, TouchID and so forth.

It is strongly recommended you take up the options your bank provides to secure your account. Some of them may require extra work and steps in order to perform operations but the trade-off against a more secure account and protection from fraud is well worth it.

Here are some other steps you can take to secure your banking even further;

If your bank gives you the ability to set transaction limits, set your limits to what is reasonable for you. If you hardly ever use your credit-card overseas, set the limit for overseas purchases to be very low. If you pay your accounts by debit or stop-order transactions and do very few manual payments, lower your payment limits from electronic channels. You have to make these decisions based on what you do, and any future plans you have.

Don't be too quick to dismiss messages from your Banking Apps or SMS. They could contain an alert of possible fraud on your account.

Don't share your banking passwords with anyone else, and don't use devices you don't own to login to your banking websites or install banking Apps.

Set a strong banking password even if you are using biometrics such as FaceID or TouchID. When these fail, the system falls back to your password, which needs to be very strong. (See Chapter 5: Passwords)

Keep your Bank's contact numbers handy so that you can phone them immediately if you suspect anything like fraud on your bank accounts.

Contactless Bank Cards

Contactless Bank Cards (also known as Tap-To-Pay or Tap-And-Pay cards) are a technology embedded into some bank and credit cards that allows one to pay for services without physically giving the card to anyone or inserting it into a machine. Using NFC (Near-Field Communications) one simply has to bring the card near a reader (by "tapping" it) and the card details are read over the air and used to process the transaction.

One of the biggest risks with contactless bank cards is that one can scan the card and obtain the relevant payment information without the user knowing about it. Note, however, that the proximity of the transmission is usually very close, hence for a criminal to steal money from your contactless bank cards the following would need to happen:

A credit-card machine with a transaction ready to process is brought near your card, wallet or pocket and gets close enough to read your card and process the transaction. This would need to be very close to you to work.

A specially built NFC or other technology radio receiver can be hidden and then brushed past your card to clone its data by reading the card details like a normal credit-card machine would. Again, this requires close proximity to your card.

To protect yourself, the following steps should be taken:

Check with your bank whether limits on "Tap-To-Pay" transactions can be set. Many banks allow you to have one limit for card swipes or "inserts" to read the chip with your pin, and another limit for contactless transactions. If you try to perform a contactless payment over the limit, the card machine will require the card to be inserted or swiped physically.

In addition to the above, your Bank may allow a PIN to be required for contactless payments over a certain amount. This way, small purchases like a Coffee or Burger can be done easily by just tapping the card, whereas something expensive, or a higher amount, will require a PIN to be entered after you tap the card.

Looking back to Chapter 2, remember that Phishing, Smishing and Vishing are common and actively used forms of attacks that try to get access to your bank account or credit-card information. Always be on the lookout for these types of attacks.

Your Take-Away for Chapter 3

- Use the services provided by your Bank to secure your online and digital banking products. Understand that Banks put these extra controls in place to protect you.
- Set your banking limits according to what you need, don't just max out all limits to make it easier.
- Use your contactless bank card carefully, and always keep it close to you and be aware of anyone trying to scan it. I have tested some NFC-blocking wallets and bags and some of these do work, but don't put all your faith in a wallet, purse or bag claiming it provides 100% protection against someone scanning your card.

VIRUSES AND MALWARE

What is a Virus?

There are many opinions as to what is considered the first computer virus. That depends largely on whether you are looking at the first virus on old DEC computers, UNIVAC machines, Apple II or the first IBM PCs.

A Virus in computing terms refers to a malicious program written to self-replicate and move from one computer (using the term loosely) to another. A Virus is generally written to do some kind of harm or damage, although many viruses were created just to be a nuisance. Original viruses written for the systems mentioned above, were more a case study of how to get a piece of code to move across systems and try to remain relatively difficult to remove. Viruses should be able to dodge attempts to delete them. Due to its nature of not being something easy to remove, the opposite of a Virus was invented: The Antivirus.

There have always been conspiracy theories about Virus vs Antivirus, with some people claiming that for Antivirus programs to exist, someone needs to keep writing viruses. A finger is sometimes pointed to the Antivirus companies themselves, however there has never been any real proof of such (and computer viruses have been around for a long time).

As computers or PC's started to find themselves in more and more corporate environments, viruses were created to infect them. Through the 1980s various viruses were created, as well as more information and even frameworks on how to create viruses and infect other programs were created. Also, in the middle-to-late 80s came viruses with the intent to cause outright deletion of data. Here the Jerusalem Virus is one example. Already even back then, viruses were being used as a form of Hacktivism*, with groups or individuals trying to make social statements using viruses. As access to computers permeated more and more into society, more virus writers surfaced. The intent varied from outright malicious, to educational, fame, or just someone looking to make a statement.

Today, viruses basically accomplish the same thing they were doing back in the "old days". The goal of a virus is to infect a system through some kind of access - usually an executable - and then to infect other systems. The result is to cause some kind of damage or make a statement. The virus also tries to hide itself while looking for ways to replicate. Since viruses follow certain behavioural patterns, Antivirus companies have been very effective at creating antivirus programs and rules to defend against viruses. Still, viruses play a major role today and when coupled with malware or system vulnerabilities (more on those later), a virus can be quite devastating to users and companies.

Avoid Being Infected

The best way to prevent a virus from infecting you is to follow the same method you would to prevent a biological virus from infecting you. Don't hang around sick people, don't eat or share food and utensils with strangers. Wash hands regularly, and don't put your fingers near your face if you haven't washed them. The list goes on, but what I want to point out is that this is not so different from what you need to do to keep your computer, phone or tablet safe.

Installing programs from sources you are not sure of, or that seem too good to be true, are like allowing a stranger to hug you when they're clearly sick and are showing symptoms of having a virus. This includes downloading programs that offer something for "free" when in fact everyone else would charge for such a program. Generally, when you're being offered something that should cost a lot of money for free, be wary. When visiting sites on the internet and looking for software to download, do some research on it first, check sites like Google for information. For example, if the program you want to download is called "Bob's Cool App", go to Google and search for *"review of Bob's Cool App"* or *"how safe is Bob's Cool App"*. This can help you get information from other sources about what you want to download.

If in doubt, rather err on the side of caution and do not download something you think could infect your computer. It is also a very good idea to ensure you have a valid, up-to-date Antivirus program running. There are many out there and it is not the purpose of this book to review them. However, I do recommend you research which Antivirus is good for you and remember that "Free" is not always "good". There is a reason something is free and it may be missing a vital function you need from an Antivirus program. Research them carefully. Ask other people you know what they use and what has worked well for them. When in doubt, stick to something with a reputable global brand.

Although generally no one ever admits it, people download from not-so-savoury websites. Yes, here I'm talking about the "free movies", "free series" or "free applications" sites that go by all sorts of names but are generally known as pirate sites, warez or "torrents". I use torrents in quotes because a torrent is actually a data transfer technology, it does not in itself refer to stolen data or copyright movies and so forth. The fact remains though that many people use torrents for downloading stolen material. This makes it a very lucrative platform for malicious users to distribute malware, viruses and the like. You download from these sites at your own risk, and remember that doing so could get you in trouble with local authorities as well as having a nasty virus or malware program running around your computer. If in doubt, avoid using these sites.

Email is another very effective means for distributing dangerous programs. We covered how to protect ourselves from phishing emails and the same applies to viruses and malware. If somebody sends you a very important program, you do not have to run it. Check what it is first. Understand why the email was sent to you. Is it really claiming to be what it says? Your bank will never send you your bank statements as executables files. By executable files we mean files with an extension (*for example bankstatement.exe*) of ".exe", ".vbs", ".js", ".java" and so forth. These files generally only require you to double-click them in your mail client to run them. Thankfully, these days almost all Antivirus programs would warn you when trying to run an executable from an email. Hopefully your email provider also blocks such files as this is a basic thing to do and should be done by any serious email provider.

Be aware of ZIP files and other compressed archives as well. They could be hiding a virus or malware inside the compressed container file. If you don't know the source of the file, rather do not open it at all. If you have to, make sure your Antivirus is running or right-click the file and click the option to scan the file. Most Antivirus programs let you right-click on a file and will have an option such as "Scan with..." or "Scan this file" and so forth. If your Antivirus does not have that option directly from your email application, save the file to disk such as in the Downloads folder and then try to right-click the file. Remember to delete the file if your antivirus finds something or just do not save it at all if you're suspicious of it. Rather let a legitimate person contact you again, or phone you to ask why you did not act on a file, than open a file you think might be suspect and land-up finding out the hard way that it was actually a virus or malware.

I often get asked which the best Antivirus program is to use. I don't support one or another particular program. I suggest two things: Firstly, get an Antivirus program that is well known and reputable. This does not mean it's expensive, or even paid-for. Research articles that compare Antivirus programs and find the one you need. Secondly, don't assume that an Antivirus program is 100% guaranteed. They can come very close to that, but there is no such thing as perfect security. Even if an Antivirus program does not pick-up viruses or malware, if you are suspicious about the source of a file you received, found or downloaded - just delete it.

Your Take-Away for Chapter 3

- Viruses have been in existence for a long time. Although initially intended to prove a point and perform mischievous actions, viruses are now used largely for malicious purposes or to spread other malware used to perform further tasks.
- Do not just install software or run programs, especially from emails, without investigating what they are and who sent them. Use an anti-virus program to assist you in identifying possibly dangerous software.
- "FREE" is not always better. Do your research on which Antivirus system will work for you, and your budget.

PASSWORDS

You used Password123 Didn't you?!

Passwords are everywhere. We use them to access our mobile devices, to access our email, social media, banking, shopping, and the list goes on and on. Passwords are also here to stay. Despite many people claiming that new technologies are going to replace passwords, years come, and years go - and passwords continue to be around. What's worse, they are also a major contributor to breached systems, breached user accounts and theft of data, identities and money. Passwords seem to be something we all hate. We forget them, we can never make them strong enough and generally we just re-use the same one that works for us.

I'm hoping that is now history for you! From today you will be choosing better, stronger and more useful passwords. I'm going to explain why this is necessary and how you can do it. We will also touch upon Password Managers - applications designed to generate and store highly secure passwords for you.

To start, let's consider some common passwords people use. Password123? Password@123? June@2018 (or <month>@<year>)? Your birthdate? Your children' or pets' (if you have) names or birthdates? Your address? Your phone number? Have you ever used any of these as a password? If you have you are not alone as millions of people do this every single minute of every day. Maybe you use a combination of these, such as Birthdate+Childs name. So, you have for example *201198Johnny*. I'm sorry to disappoint you but that is not a strong password at all. In fact, to "crack" that password would take very little effort in terms of combining digits and alpha characters. Not only that, but how hard is it for someone to find out your child's name and your birthdate? Chances are a few minutes of looking at your Facebook profile and they can already have figured that out, let alone any other means of finding that information.

Remember that data is the most important aspect here. As I mentioned right at the beginning of the book, data is everything. Passwords protect data. However, passwords are also data in themselves. Not treating them properly puts everything else at risk. Do you share your passwords with your friends, family or fellow employees? Every time you give your password to someone you put the data it protects at risk.

You also reveal how you choose passwords. If you give someone your password of *"July@2018"* - just to use quickly, next month they probably have a very good idea of what your next password is.

Let's take a look now at how to choose secure passwords. It's not hard to do and I'll show you some easy ways to train yourself to pick strong and secure passwords. Remember too, a password is yours. As with anything private or secret, you don't share it with others!

Secure passwords are possible

How to choose secure passwords depends largely on the amount of effort you want to put in. If you don't care much about your data, you will put in minimal effort and thus generally pick weak passwords. If, however, you've learnt something from this book already and you value the importance of your data, you will put some effort into choosing stronger, effective passwords.

Stronger passwords are more difficult to crack. When we speak about cracking a password, we are referring to the art of taking a securely stored password, which we call a "hash" and recovering the matching plain-text password used to generate it. What is a hash? When systems store passwords, a common (and better) method is to take your plain text password, such as *"Password123"*, and convert it using a one-way transformation into a non-identifiable version of your password. These one-way transformations involve various complex mathematical functions depending on how strong the "hash" is. For example, an MD5 hash representation of *"Password123"* is *42f749ade7f9e195bf475f37a44cafcb* (Ps: MD5 is a terribly insecure hashing algorithm, but you get the point of what a hash is). It is supposed to prevent passwords stored in databases from being easily retrieved by a hack or data leak. In many cases it does, but if your password is also weak you contribute to making it much easier to crack. Note that complexity for hashing passwords may include a "salt" or additional characters as a means of ensuring a hash is harder to crack but that is not part of our discussion.

CHANGING PASSWORDS OFTEN DOES NOT MAKE YOU MORE SECURE

If you want to choose a secure password, here is a list of things you should **never** base your password on:

Your name and/or surname.

Your children or pets' names.

Your birthdate or the birthdate of any family member including pets.

The current month, year, or any date combination that is identifiable to you.

Your company name, company address, website and so forth.

Your mobile number, telephone number or social security number (ID)

I know what you're thinking! "But's what's left for me to base my password on?!". Yes, it is true that the list above rules out a lot of things you remember easily. However, that is the whole point. Things that are easily known about you can also be easily known by someone else. Additionally, when people are looking to crack a password, they will use dictionaries containing common words, dates, numbers and so forth. Additionally, password cracking tools have powerful rule engines that can generate or manipulate words in real-time to match certain patterns.

So, how do you ensure a password is strong, secure and cannot be easily cracked should your data be leaked? We will consider three things you can do to make your password strong. First is password length. Second is password complexity, and third is password structure.

Password Length

The length of your password is important. Should your password hash value be leaked, the speed at which attackers can crack your password is directly proportional to its length. For this reason, choosing a password below 10 characters is just not acceptable in this day and age. Even if the company domain, website or other system allows you to choose a password below 10 characters, resist the urge to do so. The longer the password, the better for you.

Of course, you need to find that sweet spot between what length is secure vs what you can actually remember. A password of 64 characters is awesome, but what are the chances you're able to enter it 20 times a day at various sites and systems? (Later on, we'll discuss Password Managers which can help with this). For this reason, stick to a length you can work with. Can you remember 20 characters? Perfect! Use that, but remember it's not just length, its about complexity and structure. Which brings us to the next item;

Password Complexity

It is pointless to have a nice long password of say 12 characters but the password is "*123456789000*" - because that is simple to crack or guess. This is where complexity comes in. Not only does password length make it harder for people to guess your password - complexity adds even more difficulty. When choosing the complexity of your password, try to add characters you would not normally use in general writing of words. For example, you could choose a password of "*loPsdAfgh*". What's better than that? Adding some numeric and non-alpha characters. Let's try this one based on the previous password: "*loP23s(dA$fgh*". What you have done now is added more complexity by adding digits and special characters. Ideally your password should always contain a mixture of all of the below;

Upper- and lower-case alpha characters (A-Z, a-z)

Digits (0-9)

Special Characters or non-alpha characters (#$%! etc)

Emojis - yes you can use Emojis in passwords! but some websites or systems may not allow you to, so if it fails when choosing your password leave them out and stick to the first 3 above.

Password Structure

Your password should have a good and strong structure. What this means is that you should avoid certain "human" tendencies that make passwords weaker. These are;

Using digits in sequence such as 123, or 012 and so forth.

Using sentences that make grammatical sense, for example "*thecatjumpedover*".

Using passwords with a structure from freely available sources. For example, "*Matthew24:14*" has upper and lower case, digits and a special character - But it is a password based on a Bible book and verse and that structure is well known to password cracking methodologies.

When choosing the structure of your password be random - but remember something that works for you. For example, think to yourself that from now on every password I create will always have a structure of: "5 mixed letters, 2 numbers and 4 special characters". Further, think to yourself that your password will be a sentence you remember, but only every 2nd character in that sentence. The sentence could be "I love to go riding". Therefore using the above your password could be *"(lvtgrdnOO23)! *"* - that's 11 characters and has a good complexity and structure. You will find that in time it will be easier to remember more complex passwords because you force yourself to do so. Our brains are very capable of remembering complex passwords, we just need to force it to do so! Don't be afraid to use sentences as passwords but remember not to rely on the sentence itself as the complexity of your password.

Don't overdo password complexity and structure either, as this will also result in you forgetting passwords. Find a good balance between all of the above and you will be successful in having strong passwords. You should, however, consider using a Password Manager. We will now discuss what these can do for you and why you should use them.

Password Managers

A password manager is software used to generate and store highly secure passwords. Since it is almost impossible to remember a unique, strong and complex password for every website, a password manager makes this possible. It also prevents you from using the same password over and over on different sites. With a password manager you can have a strong password for your Facebook account and then a strong but completely different password for your Gmail or Yahoo! accounts.

A password manager uses a vault to securely store your password. Like a safe - you then have one very strong, very secure and complex password to remember - that unlocks the vault containing all your other passwords. The program then automatically fills-in passwords for you once your vault is unlocked. This means you only need to remember one very secure and very complex password to secure the main vault. All other passwords are "remembered" by the program in that vault.

To learn more, check out one example of a password manager: 1Password. You'll find information on it here: https://1password.com/tour/

You will find that using a password manager helps you to have far more secure passwords. There are password manager apps for your phone, tablet, computer and even just in your browser so you are never without your vault of secure passwords. Remember though, like any safe, your master password for your password manager must be kept extremely safe, secure and complex!.

Stronger passwords will make it harder for people with malicious intent to access your data. It won't make it impossible, since you are still relying on the technology of website and system owners to be secure as well, but even if they are not - the better your password, the less chance of it being cracked, guessed or brute-forced.

Your Take-Away for Chapter 5

- You use passwords everywhere, and hence they are a critical part of keeping yourself secure.
- Choose complex, long passwords that you will not easily forget.
- If it is up to you, do not change passwords too often. Just make sure you have very secure ones.
- Password Managers are your friends. Find a good, reliable one and use it properly. It will elevate the quality of passwords you use and make it less likely you will forget complex passwords.
- Avoid using dictionary-based words in passwords, names of family, pets, dates, address information and so forth.

VPNS

What is a VPN?

The word VPN stands for Virtual Private Network. As its name implies, it is the use of a private network over a public network (such as the Internet) but it is created virtually. That is, it is not a physical network connection - since to have a physical private network you would need to physically connect to different locations. The VPN gives you your own private connection over an existing public connection by creating a virtual network on top of the current public one.

To illustrate, think of sending a locked box via Post to another location. The Post Office service is the public service, in this case anything you send is mixed with all the other general mail items. However, an envelope in the locked box would not be seen by anyone at the Post office because they cannot access the locked box. In this case, you have a private mail service inside that locked box because you can send envelopes with important information inside the box and all the Post Office will ever see is a box they move around, not what is inside it. Only when it gets delivered at the end can that person open the box and see the secret envelope inside.

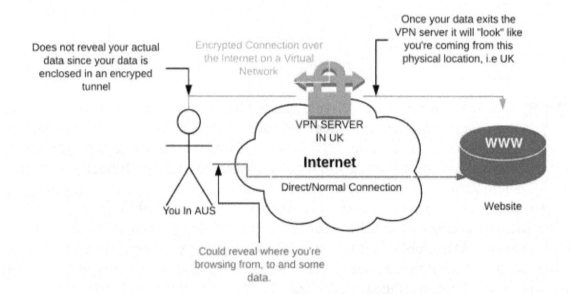

A VPN does the same thing, it encrypts your information and creates a secure tunnel between yourself and another party, using the public internet as the transport. Through that tunnel, you can send any data you want, and it will not be seen by anyone along the way. Additionally, wherever your VPN connects to is where your internet connection will appear to be coming from. For example, if you live in Australia (AUS in the image), but connect to a VPN network who's VPN server is in the United Kingdom (UK), and you browse to a website over the VPN, the website will think you're coming from the United Kingdom because that is where your VPN exits and your connection goes back onto the public internet.

A VPN can also exit inside a corporate network. This allows you to use the internet as the carrier but appear as though you are connected to the office. All your data is encrypted and sent over the Internet to the VPN server which then sends your data out into the internal network as if it were originating from there. Initially, VPNs were primarily used to give employees access to corporate offices via the Internet and the use of such systems was expensive, and the methods of authentication (proving who you are) was often done using expensive One-Time-Pin devices. As the Internet became more commonplace in society and technology became cheaper and more available, VPNs became easier to create and manage. Further, companies were born whose sole goal is to sell VPN access to allow you to connect from one location over a secure link to another location.

VPNs have become very common in countries with strict national control over the Internet. Where certain services are banned for users in those countries, a VPN would bypass that problem since it creates an encrypted sub-network over the existing one in which the country's firewalls and data analysis cannot see what is being sent or received, so they cannot block it. Be warned however that this does not mean VPNs are a golden answer to using the Internet freely in restrictive countries. Many countries that restrict Internet use also have laws banning the use of VPNs. If you are caught with a VPN connection that can be traced back to you, you could be in trouble. Always do your research first to understand what and why certain restrictions apply in certain countries.

For most of the world however, VPNs are allowed and sometimes even encouraged. If you connect to a public Wi-Fi network, I strongly recommend enabling a VPN and then browsing the Internet through that. Public Wi-Fi is rarely encrypted which means people can see what you're doing and possibly attack you with certain means to try to steal your browser information, passwords and more. A VPN makes it much harder for a malicious person to access your data or attack your connection compared to browsing over an open Wi-Fi connection because the VPN is an encrypted tunnel that the attacker cannot easily access to view the data.

What about SSL? Do I need a VPN?

Remember not to rely on a VPN as being the only secure way to access the Internet. Websites and services use SSL that encrypts communications between them and your browser. SSL, or Secure Sockets Layer, is the standard method for encrypting data between a client (your browser or application) and the server (a website or a service on the Internet). This is the primary method of securing data between users and web servers. However, in some cases SSL is not used, or you want to access a service that would normally not be allowed from your location - that is when a VPN comes in handy. Further, you might be connected to non-encrypted public Wi-Fi networks such as at hotels and restaurants where, even with SSL, it is still a generally good idea to use an encrypted transport for all your Internet usage. A VPN will do that for you.

What is SSL then?

When you open a browser and connect to a website, you may sometimes notice that the browser address shows HTTP:// or sometimes it shows HTTPS://. The "S" on the latter indicates an SSL-secured HTTP connection to the server. This means that data sent between you and the server will be encrypted. To illustrate, think of a conveyor carrying something between two points. The conveyor is open on either end so whatever you put into the one will move to the other side at the receiving party. Anyone watching the conveyor can see what moves across it. This is what the HTTP protocol does - it delivers website content from the web server to your browser. It is possible if one is intercepting the traffic to see what either end is sending or receiving. Now, however, imagine we enclose the conveyor in a large pipe with locked doors on either end. The only way to put something on the conveyor now is to unlock it from one side, and the only way to get the items out of the other end of the conveyor is to unlock that side and open the door. A key is required on both ends and only the parties on either end with a valid key can unlock the doors to access what is on the conveyor. Also, since it is now enclosed you can't see what is being transported on the conveyor.

This is what SSL does for HTTP - it ensures a secured pipe (or transport) when delivering content from the web server to your browser. Somebody in between cannot access the data since it's encrypted in transit - much like the conveyor's content is protected inside the locked pipe when in transit.

To ensure you are being adequately protected by an SSL secured session, you have to make sure of certain points;

Your browser should **not** display an error next to the HTTPS:// address (on the left you will see a padlock usually indicating the SSL session. It should have no exclamation marks or alerts).

If you browse to a website and your browser prompts you to say there is an SSL Error, or a Secure Connection could not be established because of an SSL Certificate error - proceed with caution. This means your browser is being told it has a secure connection to the server but could not verify it. Your browser relies on a unique and valid cryptographic certificate to initiate an SSL connection to the server. If someone is trying to intercept your connection it often gets detected this way because they are trying to send you an invalid certificate. By clicking Proceed or Accept - you are telling your browser to ignore the warnings. **This could allow your secure data to be decrypted or monitored**. Of course, if the website owner simply configured SSL incorrectly, you would get the same error so don't be too quick to assume an SSL error on a website means you're under attack. It simply means you should be careful because the website may not be what it claims to be, or your data in transit could be visible to attackers.

Any reputable website (in fact, almost all websites) should have an SSL certificate and when you access it in your browser there should be an indication that it is secure. This is especially true for any website where you need to provide login information, personal information, credit-card information and so forth. Avoid submitting such information to a website without SSL security (i.e. running as HTTP only).

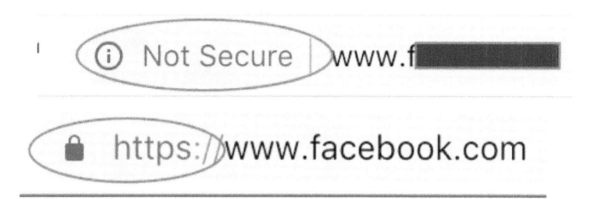

Here we have an example of how a browser identifies secure (HTTPS) websites vs non-secure (HTTP) websites; non-secure connection and secure connection (second picture)

Note that some browsers may simply display a padlock indicating the security level. No padlock means no encryption, a padlock with a line through it or an exclamation mark means there is an SSL certificate and you're using HTTPS but there is a problem with the encryption (i.e. you are being warned it may not be legitimate) or just a padlock indicating a normal secured connection.

It was previously an expensive exercise to get an SSL Certificate for a website, but these days it is cheap and rather simple to implement. Therefore, there is no reason most websites should be serving their pages over HTTPS.

Your Take-Away for Chapter 6

- VPNs are designed to protect all traffic flowing between two points.
- A VPN can be used to bypass country-imposed content restrictions (at your own risk!) or to make your internet traffic appear to be coming from a particular location - where your VPN "terminates".
- A VPN can allow you to connect to the internal network of your company/employer from the Internet.

- SSL or Secure Sockets Layer is like a pipe that protects the HTTP traffic flowing between web servers and your browser.
- You can tell if you're using a secure website as it will have an HTTPS address and/or a padlock depending on the browser used.

SOCIAL MEDIA

Socialite or Social Fright?

Whether you are a social media addict, or simply have social media accounts so people don't think you have forgotten what decade we're in - sooner or later you will ask the question that ultimately everybody does;

How do I keep safe on Social Media?

Many years ago, if you wanted to share photos with your friends or family, you would put them in an envelope and send them each a copy. Fast-forward a few years and you still had to do a similar thing with your photos but with the advent of e-mail, you could easily attach your now digital photo to messages to each person (or get fancy with CC and BCC lists). There was still a hole, however, regarding one's social life. While email and the odd news board on the internet were ways, we could get our information out, short of building our own websites we did not have somewhere for anyone to just "consume" social information about us without us needing to purpose-fully ensure we were sending it to them. You could chat in real-time with ICQ, IRC, AOL Messenger and, lest we not forget, MSN Messenger.

Something was missing, however, and although a few sites like SixDegrees.com tried to bring social networking to the masses, it was in 2004 with the launch of Facebook that social networking really took a major upward turn. It became popular, normal, "the-in-thing" and generally just very easy for humans to start sharing their lives online. A quick photo, a quick thought, where you're at - all of this could be updated easily in one place and the friends and family (or strangers) you chose to access it could easily keep track of you. Further, it allowed friends and family who may have not seen each other for years to finally have a platform to connect and re-unite.

YOUR LIFE, NOW ON SALE

A key point to remember with almost any social media or social networking site is that they exist for multiple reasons but ultimately 2 purposes: To make money, and to provide a service to the public. The two are of course inter-related, since a website or service that the public enjoys using will also be one that generates good revenue.

The question that seemed to slip many peoples' minds for a long time however, was : "How are social networking sites making money, often without advertising and without subscription models?"

The short answer and the one that for many years went unnoticed is that social networking companies were selling data to other parties. Think about your social media account for a moment. Chances are the following information is available or has been captured by you on such systems:

Your full name and surname.

Your mobile or telephone number.

Your physical address (more on this below).

Your family - by linking them as family members on the system.

Your photos (see below on photo information).

Your employment status, marital or relationship status and mood status.

Your location or location history and much more.

That is a LOT of information. And information is money. Just think if you are a retail giant knowing which status updates of the public include your store's name. Did someone say they're going to buy something from you? Or perhaps knowing who has been in your store from location data and then correlating that to persons, age groups, personalities, family type and so forth. Information is extremely valuable but was it more valuable is when someone can tie multiple sources of information together to paint a picture.

Enter Cambridge Analytica. For years, Facebook sort of ran below the radar of an all-out accusation of selling their users data. There was suspicion, and some incidents here and there. However, nothing concrete came to light, until March 2018. It was revealed through media agencies and through an ex-employee, that Facebook had given the data of millions of people to Cambridge Analytica, a company specialising in data analysis and correlation - in this instance - for political analysis and resale to political parties.

All in all, it is estimated that about "up to 87 million users'" data was given to Cambridge Analytica. That number comes from Facebook itself, hence there is a reasonable possibility it is actually higher.

The point is not to discuss selling of data but to highlight the importance of data. If a multi-billion-dollar company like Facebook saw the value in sharing personal information, and in turn another provider sells it for financial gain, **you can be assured that malicious entities want your data just as much, if not more.**

Think for a minute now on how many social media sites, or social networking sites and/or related companies have been hacked over time and had data leaked? No doubt our personal information such as what I mentioned above is also leaked. That data can be sold on the Internet easily.

Here is a list of some uses for stolen or leaked data from a hacked social networking website;

- Creation of false identities by stealing real names - coupled with real addresses and even photos - that is, Identity Theft.
- Phishing scams using real names and other information considered "true" about the persons to generate trust.
- Paedophile activities and related malicious intent such as identifying children and their location, or family names and so forth.
- Blackmail due to leaked photographs or information that should not have been made public.

The list goes on and on. But you get the idea. Your data is valuable, as we saw in Chapter 1.

Of course, Social Media and Networking is not going to go away. The primary reason is we are social beings, and, despite the negative points, Social sites and apps provide us with enjoyment and entertainment. They can offer much good, and as such, will be around for a long, long time.

Let's discuss how to keep ourselves secure on these systems, to ensure that even if data is sold, or stolen, we minimise the impact to ourselves.

Be Socially Secure

As we have seen, much information is available to both corporate and malicious entities that can be used for purposes we may not approve of. How do we maintain proper balance so that we can enjoy Social Media and Networking but also still remain secure?

Share What You Need To - Not What You're Asked To

When a site asks you to enter your personal information, think about **why** and **what.** Why do they want your address? Facebook, for example, can work perfectly well without your physical address listed on it. So why share that? The same applies to many other websites and applications of a similar nature. Oversharing of information is a common cause of identity theft, and increases one's risk as a target to phishing, because the more we give out and share, the less control we have over it. The same applies to mobile numbers and email addresses. Granted, such are often needed to register for certain sites and services, however there is rarely ever a need to make such information publicly viewable.

The table below shows some examples of what you might want to share online, and whether or not it is advisable to do so. Keep in mind we are referring to sharing such information publicly or making it "viewable" on your profile on any social network site.

My Personal Information	Should I Share It?
Physical or work address	No. There is never a need for the public to see your physical address.
Mobile or fixed-line phone number	No. There is rarely ever a need for the public to see this information. Send it privately to those you want to share it with.
Photographs - General/ Vacations/Selfies	Share with caution. Don't share more than you need to and avoid sharing photos that fully identify your location. Remember, photos from a mobile device or some cameras often contain location information as well that sites can extract even though it is not displayed.
Photographs - Children	Generally, no. Share with EXTREME caution. Especially photographs showing possible location of children.

	Also, considering locking down your profile to only allow friends and people you absolutely trust to view these photos. Photos of children could show a malicious person who they are, what they like, how many children are in the family, possible friends, locations they are often at and so forth. Get the point?
Location Information	"Check-in" is a nice way to show people where you are. It is also a nice way to be profiled or allow unsavoury persons to know what you're up to and when. Limit location sharing to only friends and family (by securing your profile). Additionally, try choosing a general location. For example: *New York.* Instead of: *No X, XYZ East Street, New York.*
Status Updates	For some of us, it is important to let people know what we're doing every 5 minutes. Don't judge! However, try to limit the information to not allow a perfectly clear picture of your life and daily activities and habits to be profiled.
Family Links	Limit the sharing of family links - that is linking family member's social media accounts to yours and displaying the information publicly. This allows a person who can see your profile to easily figure out your family structure, children's names etc.
Credit-Cards, Bank Checks and Boarding Passes	No. Absolutely never share pictures of these publicly and there is probably

	absolutely no reason to have them in a private gallery on your social networking sites anyway. Remember, a barcode on a boarding pass can be scanned to get your flight details including itinerary, frequent-flyer information, passport information (if pre-captured) and so forth. Avoid sharing photos of boarding pass slips.

The above list may seem restrictive at first but with time, and by understanding the data involved, it will become second nature to you. After checking what we are posting and sharing, we soon become more aware, even subconsciously, to what we are seeing. This allows for quick action and simply re-composing a frame or choosing not to share a photo we've taken. The same applies to status updates and locations and so forth.

Your Take-Away for Chapter 7

- Social Media and Social Networking sites have been around for a while, but exponentially increased in popularity in recent years. This means they also have become more popular for attackers.
- As with anything "free" - you must know and understand what data about you will be shared, processed, or sold by social companies.
- The more you share about yourself publicly, the more info a malicious person has to use when trying to scam or attack you electronically.
- Be careful what you post online, use the table above as a reminder of the risks regarding what you post.

CHILDREN AND CYBER SECURITY

Kids, The Internet, And You

There is no shortage of games, educational websites, activities and videos available on the Internet for kids. As each year goes by, and each decade, we see younger and younger individuals using the Internet. If you want proof, just ask an 8-year-old how to do something on your mobile phone - there's a very good chance they already know!

To simply cut off the Internet from young ones is a harsh, and rarely successful way to keep a young person off the internet. No doubt you want the best for your kids without compromising their safety. To do this, we will consider three important aspects and discuss them:

1. Empowering your child to *understand* threats on the Internet.
2. What you can do as a *Parent* to secure your child on the Internet.
3. How *technology* can secure your child on the Internet.

Let's focus first on empowering your child. What does this mean? Children do not have a full understanding of the world around them. They tend to trust people more than adults do, and they take things at face value. This puts them at risk for cyber security attacks that can span simple phishing, to coercion, brainwashing as well as targets for paedophiles. You can't teach your child 20 years of experience in a few hours, neither can you - or should you - expect them to think like an adult. What you can do, however, is explain things to them in a manner that they understand. A child has the ability, although basic, to understand how their data is important to them. Take for example their toys. If you ask a child whether you can give away their favourite toy, what will be their answer? Probably "No!". The reason is the toy has value to them and they do not want to lose it. Try now to associate that with something they should not give away on the Internet. Ask them, "If somebody you don't know on the Internet asks you to give them your toy, will you give it?" Again, their reply would probably be "No!". Now expand that to the related but important data. Ask the child "Okay, so if a stranger on the Internet asks where you live, would you tell them? Because they want to come and steal your favourite toy!" What you have done now is created an association in their minds that giving out information on the Internet can lead to a loss of something they desire, cherish and appreciate.

When it comes to avoiding coercion, brainwashing and other propaganda, it is slightly more difficult. We are not going to delve into psychology and religious upbringing in this book, however, suffice it to say that a direct result of how easy it will be for a malicious person to coerce or brainwash your child depends on their upbringing. Children who feel secure, who can open up to parents and who have had an understanding of certain morals instilled in them would be harder to influence. Isolated children, and children who have very poor communication channels with their parents make excellent targets since they are more prone to keeping secrets. Either way, however, a skilled person could have at least some success in luring a child or teenager in any circumstance.

What can you do as a parent to secure your child? Visibility of what your child is doing on the Internet can go a long way towards looking for signs that something is wrong. Do not confuse this with "spying" on your children. There is a difference between prying and knowing. Of course, a young child has less understanding of privacy and is less concerned with their own privacy, so it is easier to have a more hands-on approach to knowing their Internet usage. However, older children and teenagers start to understand and value privacy. This is where you need to have good communication channels and also look for serious signs that your child may be affected by something on the Internet.

I'm going to touch for a moment on an article in the news about two years ago, that discussed knowing whether your child is a "hacker". The article mentioned that if your child spends an extraordinary amount of time in their room on the computer, knows a few programming languages, prefers to chat to friends online and shows signs of hate towards, or a negative attitude towards, authorities and governments, that they could be a "hacker".

I found this to be rather extreme. Firstly, the term "hacker" actually does not, by definition, denote a criminal or malicious person. *It is the actions of a hacker that dictate whether they are malicious or not.* Would you call surgeons criminals? No. But a surgeon specialising in the black-market trade of organs is a criminal. Therefore, it is not the skill of being a surgeon that is criminal, it is what they do with their skills.

In the purest definition, a "hacker" is a person who questions and pushes the boundaries of technology. They ask the "Why? Who? What?" when it comes to anything they see. A hacker would look at something and wonder about how it **doesn't** work. Not about how we're expected to use it. Mainstream use of the term "hacker" in recent decades however has associated it with criminal or illegal activity.

The point is that if your child is very interested in technology, programming languages, and so forth do not assume they're trying to hack into the F.B.I. There is nothing wrong with learning and being inquisitive. It could be their career choice, their future, and their passion to work with technology - even as a "hacker" - one that is not actually doing harm, stealing or destroying anything. The term "ethical hacker" was coined to differentiate between those who hack maliciously vs those who have the skill to benefit others. Pity we didn't enforce career terms like "ethical surgeon" and "ethical lawyer" too...

Coming back to our main point here: Understand what your child is doing online. Ask questions that help you understand the attitude of your child. Talk to them about their internet activity. Ask them what they are interested in doing online. Maintain enough communication so that if they do ever get involved in something by mistake or through coercion or influence by a third party, they will be more inclined to seek your assistance and guidance on the matter.

Finally, how can technology help? There are a plethora of tools, programs and subscriptions you can take out to control Internet usage. It is up to you, as well as your responsibility as a parent, to figure out what to control and how you want to control it. Software that prevents access-to and communication-from known malicious sites, extortion sites and other malicious sources can be of great value. They can act as a good first line of defence in catching anything that could pose a threat to your child. The same applies to mobile phones on which there are many programs and features too.

Most mobile phones also allow for age restriction locks these days. If your young child has a phone, you probably purchased it. You have the right, and the responsibility, to lock it down as necessary in order to protect your child.

Consider the following options for securing devices your child uses;

Option	What it does?
Age Restriction on Media Apps	Almost all applications that stream media, music and movies allow for age-restricted locks to be implemented. Check with your app provider on your child's account. Or consider a family account where you can also configure these settings yourself (since you will probably be paying for it anyway).
Content-Control Software	Software such as Net Nanny can be used to control some or all of a device. The primary

	purpose is to prevent purposeful or accidental browsing of illegal, pornographic or other malicious sites and offers useful features such as instant alerts if a child searches a certain topic. There are other options available so look around for what works for you.
Time Lock Apps	There are many time lock apps for devices that allow you to force lock the device during certain periods (such as sleep time, study time etc). Although not really security-related, these can also solve some problems such as your kids grades by limiting the amount of time on non-essential activities instead of studying or doing homework.
Antivirus Apps	Antivirus (including Anti-Malware and other suites) can ensure the device does not pick up any unwanted and dangerous applications. Since mobile phones, and to an extent tablets, normally have GPS, a compromised device can do more than just spread nasty messages. It can even report your Childs location, power on cameras and so forth. Generally, sticking to installing applications only from your phone's official App Store (Google Play or Apple App Store) can help prevent malicious apps. This is not a fool-proof method though. Try to also limit downloading and installing what isn't necessary and watch out for "FREE" versions of paid-for apps - they can often be clones designed to spread malware. Be aware that some antivirus applications have been known to slow down devices and/or consume more battery power, so do your homework and research which is best at this point in time and within your budget.

Another aspect of protection for your children in Cyber Security is when it comes to devices they carry with them. From IOT Toys to wearable tracking devices you need to ensure that you are not giving your child a connected device that allows hackers to track them, listen to them or worse - see them. Don't just buy devices that claim to do something without properly researching them.

In the end, one can only do so much to ensure that a child or teenager is safe on the Internet. Undue panic does not solve anything either, and neither should we ever get complacent by thinking that our actions have obtained 100% security. That does not exist. You can, however, very greatly minimise the possibility and the impact of something nasty happening by taking the right steps.

Your Take-Away for Chapter 8

- Young Children and teenagers will continue using technology, and adopt it more and more, as the future progresses. Assist them to be secure as they do this.
- There are many risks to young people using the Internet, and as someone responsible for them, you need to stay abreast of these and ensure you protect them - without undue controls that will simply drive them to find covert ways to use the technology and thus remain at risk.
- Leverage available tools and applications to help protect your young kids and teens.

I'VE BEEN HACKED!

The words nobody ever wants to hear: "I've been hacked!"

The first thing to do, and probably the very last thing you want to do right now is... don't panic! I don't say this because one should not be panicking, obviously it's a stressful time and scary event to happen to you. However, panicking rarely allows one to accomplish things in an orderly and well-thought out manner, something you need to do if you've been hacked.

Take Stock of The Situation

What exactly has happened? Find and understand the answers to the following important questions:

What hack has actually taken place? Was I phished? Has someone planted malware on my computer? Did someone use my bank card or access my bank accounts? And so forth.

Understand the loss. What have I immediately lost? This could be financial, trust-related, physical items or data.

What action must I take right **now** to stop any further loss, disable access to my machine or device, and stop attackers getting any further?

Once you know what you're dealing with, it's easier to move forward and take action. Of course, it is not expected that everyone fully understands Cybersecurity and immediately knows how they were attacked and the technical aspects therein. However, it's not hard to identify an attack, and what device is affected by it and what losses you have or may experience.

You may also have identified an attack by a defensive application alerting you to it. For example, your Antivirus tells you that something you've tried to execute on your computer contains a virus or malware. Generally, it is advisable to follow their instructions but make sure this is an actual application you installed - not just some random website popup claiming you have a virus.

Be careful, too, not to be phished through a simulated or "fake" attack. These happen a lot and many people fall for them. Someone simulates an attack, or simply contacts you to tell you you've been hacked and they magically (and from the kindness of their heart) want to help you fix the problem. In almost every case this is just another method of phishing and trying to defraud you, as at some point they'll either try to actually install malware on your device or try to get you to pay them money for a service they didn't perform. If you know someone with technical experience, contact them to help you, it is best to avoid allowing uninvited strangers to do so.

Put A Plan in Action

There are a few things you should immediately do when you confirm you have been breached through some kind of attack or hack. They are;

Isolate the device or computer from the Internet until further notice.

Change passwords on critical apps or websites you were using from the device that's compromised - do it from **a different** device. Don't change it from the same suspect device.

If you think your bank card was compromised, phone the bank or use your bank's app to temporarily block the card until you know more - again don't do these activities from the device or computer you believe to be compromised.

Take the device or computer to a trusted technical person/friend/staff-member to investigate further. In the case of mobile phones (and sometimes other devices), it is not a bad idea to do a factory reset and install from the start again. Make sure important data is backed-up (it is best to do backups before you need them).

It's Not the End of The World

These things happen to people all the time, including technically minded individuals and even security professionals, since no one is perfect. Don't assume that you should never use the Internet or any connected device ever again. Simply learn from the mistake. If this has happened to your child/teenager - help them understand how they got into that situation so that they can learn as well.

See the Quick-Guide for a step-by-step method to identify if you have been hacked and what could possibly be the outcome.

Your Take-Away for Chapter 9

Don't panic! Understand what happened, what is affected and put a plan in place.

Take action and perform necessary steps to prevent further damage and protect yourself.

This happens to many people, and while it does not excuse one for not taking steps to be secure - it means if you have been hacked it's not the end of the world. Adapt and move on.

THE INTERNET OF (NOT SO SECURE) THINGS (IOT)

The Internet of Things or IOT for short, refers to devices that have embedded systems to allow them to be connected to networks and/or the Internet. For example, if you had a Fridge and an IOT Fridge, the IOT Fridge would be one that could connect to your home Wi-Fi and be controllable via an App on your phone to check temperature, change settings and so forth. It usually involves taking disconnected devices and making them connected.

When it comes to the security of IOT devices, they unfortunately have a long and patchy history of being rather insecure. The reason is varied, but probably comes down to the very short time between design, development, and release. Many of these devices have flooded the market and security research and planning appeared to be on the afterburner. Very little effort is put into how to secure the devices themselves, the data on them and how access is controlled to the devices. This has resulted in some horror stories such as IOT Baby Monitors that random strangers were able to access or speak through. In my research I have studied some IOT devices and been able to find vulnerabilities on them too as many other security researchers have done as well. A very interesting study, the presentation of which I attended in person, was about how insecure children's tracking watches are. These IOT devices are worn by kids, record sound and location and send that data via GSM data to cloud servers. The security is very bad, and the demonstration displayed how it was possible to access the location of random children without owning the watch as well as get access to real-time sound around the children amongst other functionality.

What Do I Need to Know?

There are a few things one needs to know about any IOT device before plugging it in, joining to Wi-Fi and using it. In fact, before evening buying it.

Your IOT Device can be affected by many threats, some of which you do not have any control over. The figure below shows the threats that could affect your IOT Device and allow someone to view sensitive data, control devices or spy on you:

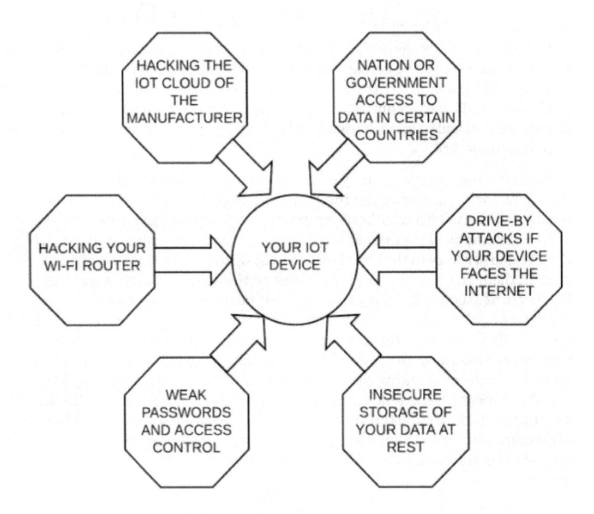

If the device has a camera or microphone, you should be aware that the data could be sent off-site from the device to cloud storage or services. This includes any ambient sound or photos/videos while the device is idle not only when it is used. There are a few things you can do to limit the security risks of these devices. Use the list below to help you:

- Research a device before you buy it. Find out what, if any, security problems may exist with the device and whether they have been patched.
- Check reviews for the device to see if any other people have had security issues.
- Use the device carefully if it has a camera or microphone and when not in use, rather turn it off. If the device will be used by children, make extra sure that the device security is up to spec. If you cannot turn it off, consider blocking the camera or turning it away from facing sensitive areas or children.

IOT Devices can also span home automation as well. These devices can control locks, room temperature, lighting, and alarm systems. The inherent risks to security carry across to these devices as well. The key is not to become paranoid and never use IOT devices. Afterall they perform some important functions for us too. For example, IOT cameras can provide security by allowing you to monitor your home when you are away and ensure safety. The problem is that vulnerabilities to your device could allow attackers to do the same.

The ability to access IOT devices as an attacker depends largely on a few factors including:

- Whether the device exposes its own web or other interface on the network or Internet.
- Whether the device communicates securely with cloud services or it uses insecure communication protocols.
- Whether the device has built-in backdoors or vulnerabilities.
- Whether the cloud service the device uses has adequate security and controls in place to protect your data and access to the devices from strangers.

Some of the above are within your control, while others are not. One thing you can do, is minimize the attack surface by not giving systems easy access to your devices via the Internet. If any device requires you to "open ports", or "map ports" or "setup a virtual service" on your router to allow Internet traffic to your IOT device, you should not do that. Most well-built IOT devices will connect-out and poll for any information they need. They should not require you to punch open holes into your network.

A similar thing to be aware of here is called UPnP (Universal Plug 'n Play). This is a protocol that allows devices to reach out to other systems on the Internet and create connections (usually over HTTP or other protocol) between the remote systems and your IOT device. The process also allows supported routers (your broadband or mobile connection device) to open incoming connections to your devices from the Internet. This can introduce risks to your environment. Further, some UPnP vulnerabilities exist in routers that can put your network at risk. It is best to disable UPnP functionality on your router or Wi-Fi Access Point Router if it is not needed.

IOT Devices are only going to grow in the world around us. As everything becomes connected and appliances and tools find their way online, we need to take the security of these systems seriously. Enjoy the functionality these devices provide for you, after all, technology is supposed to make our lives better. However, do so while ensuring IOT devices do not negatively affect the security of your data.

Your Take-Away for Chapter 10

IOT Devices can be a help in our lives and they can make us safer. However, we need to be aware of possible security risks with these devices. Always keep the following in mind:

Research the device you want to purchase properly to ensure it is secure, and at least it is made by a manufacturer who releases security updates.

Set strong passwords on the devices.

If the device is a Toy and can take video or audio, keep it packed away when not in use to minimize the amount the of sensitive data it could have access to.

Avoid allowing IOT devices to be accessed from the Internet through your router configuration or UPnP.

QUICK-GUIDE TO COMMON QUESTIONS

Hopefully you have read the entire book and then reached this point. However, even if you didn't, the section below aims to be a quick guide to help you fix common cyber security problems or events you may encounter in your life. It is by no means an A-Z of anything that can happen, however I've tried to cover most aspects and questions that we ask ourselves every day.

Passwords & Accounts

ISSUE / PROBLEM / TOPIC	RESOLUTION / ACTION
Passwords - I don't know how to choose a secure password	Keep the following in mind when choosing a password: Longer is better. Don't be afraid to think of sentences as possible passwords (many websites and systems even allow spaces for proper sentences). Aim for no less than 12 characters in your password. Include a mix of UPPER CASE, lower case, digits, and special characters like $,&,@, and others as possible. Pick long and strong passwords and don't change them too often unnecessarily. Use different passwords for different sites, and especially email/webmail. Consider a password manager like 1Password or equivalent.
I think my password was compromised/stolen/leaked	First, change the password immediately on the affected system or site and anywhere else you know you have re-used it (which you shouldn't do) Make sure you were notified about the leaked password from a reputable site and source. Just because you got an email saying your password was compromised doesn't necessarily mean it was. Ensure it came from a trusted source.
What email address should I use to register for websites, applications or anything else?	Generally, I prefer to use a "disposable" email account for signing up to services that are non-transactional (I.e financial or e-commerce) so that I don't have to put up with the spam and advertising. However, this is up to each person.

	If you don't want to manage multiple email accounts, register only where you know your email won't be re-sold or used for spam.
	TIP: Google's Gmail allows you to add a label to your email and file it accordingly. For example if you're registering on Facebook, you can use myemailaddress+facebook@gmail.com where myemailaddress@gmail.com is your actual email address but anything after the + becomes an identifiable label in your inbox when a message is sent to that address. This way you know when an email comes in, which platform it is from, because Gmail will label it with the description you used after the + and before the @gmail.com. Other email providers also offer this approach, check if yours supports it.
What if my account (i.e email address) shows up as being in a breach, or leak?	Firstly, do not panic. Almost everyone has had their email address leak somehow, somewhere. The problem is not whether it was leaked but what can somebody do with it. Look out for the following:
	Did you have a strong password set? If not, considering changing it now.
	A leaked database with "hashed" password values, i.e not the actual password text, requires such passwords to be "cracked". If the website/app owner designed their system properly they would have used hard-to-crack algorithms and configurations. Unfortunately, this is rarely the case, so there is a good chance your password will be "cracked" at some point or another. Do not use it with the associated email address of the leak anywhere else. Change it if you have done so.

Home Networking & Security

ISSUE / PROBLEM / TOPIC	RESOLUTION / ACTION
I purchased a new Router/ Broadband Router/Internet Access Device - how do I secure it?	Everyone loves to bring home that shiny new device that will give you Internet access. Be it fibre, LTE/Wireless or another method of connection. However, there are a few things you need to keep in mind; Change the default Wi-Fi password. This means the original password on the device should be used only to setup the device Wi-Fi, after that, change the Wi-Fi password to a secure password. Change the default Administrator password. Most routers need a password to let you configure them, check the manual for yours and change this password to a secure one. Disable WPS functionality. Unless absolutely needed (in which case turn it on when you actually want to use it), you should turn off WPS as it creates another possible avenue for compromise. Patch your device. Follow the manufacturer's instructions to update the software or firmware of your device to keep up to date with security fixes.
I'm investing in Home Automation. What do I need to know about security?	Home automation is an awesome technology. However, like anything else that is on a network, it can be susceptible to attacks. Ensure the software on the devices is up to date with latest patches or

revisions.

Do not allow the management systems to create Wi-Fi networks with simple passwords or "open" networks. Rather connect them to your existing secured Wi-Fi network, or create a specific secured network for them.

Research the systems you are using and stick to well-known and trusted brands and applications.

Remember, your privacy could be at risk so read the terms and conditions of everything you buy to see what they do with your data, voice, images etc.

Social Media & Social Networking

ISSUE / PROBLEM / TOPIC	RESOLUTION / ACTION
I think someone hacked my Social Media/Messaging Account	First, identify how sure you are that you have been hacked. Are posts coming from your name to other persons without you creating them? Are your contacts receiving messages or other things from your profile without you sending them? If so, immediately change your password. Also, ensure you did not give any 3rd party plugins or applications the ability to post on your behalf by accepting permissions without verifying them. Finally, contact support to log a query about your account and seek their assistance.

Web Browsing, Internet & VPN

ISSUE / PROBLEM / TOPIC	RESOLUTION / ACTION
How do I know my VPN is secure?	This is a difficult question to answer because it depends completely on the VPN provider you are using. Stick to known, reputable providers and do research on the services.
I have a VPN connected but I am still showing as browsing from my home location.	Some Operating Systems require you to check a box to force all traffic to go through the VPN. Without this option, the Operating System is trying to guess what should go where. Ensure the option is selected to force ALL your traffic over the VPN. Note however that this will stop any local network services from being usable - such as your local network printer.
When I browse websites, I keep getting notices to fix my PC, clean my PC or install other software.	You may have malware, adware or other programs in your browser that are displaying adverts. Always pay close attention to what plugins you install in your browser and remember that many "Free" ones have the side effect of randomly advertising things. If nothing else works, try re-installing the browser without inheriting previous settings or perform a scan on your system from your trusted Antivirus program.
Is it safe to shop online and give my credit-card details?	Online shopping (or e-Commerce if you will) has been around for a very long time. Much has been done to ensure the security of users shopping online but risks still exist. Keep the following in mind:

Shop online at reputable websites and stores. Always browse to the store you want to buy from and be weary of emails asking you to click a link to a store to buy something as it may not be directing you to the actual store. (That is not to say that legitimate stores don't email you, so check the links that open in your browser)

Ensure your browser has no issues with the secure session on the website, usually by not showing any exclamation marks or alerts regarding the site security.

Only put your payment details into the page opened when checking-out of the store you are buying from. Be suspicious of any emails claiming to be from stores linking you to payment pages.

Be wary of small print especially with subscription services and what money they can bill every month and so forth.

Activate your credit-card security features such as Verified-by-Visa, 3DSecure or other method used by your bank.

Your Computer, Phone, Tablet or Laptop

ISSUE / PROBLEM / TOPIC	RESOLUTION / ACTION
My Computer is very hot, and fans are always on - also my machine is slow.	Although many factors could contribute to this, you may have a "miner" installed. This is malware that uses your computer resources to mine electronic currency. As it is very hardware intensive it results in hotter systems, more power draw and overall slower system response. Use a reputable Antivirus to check your system. However, note that other factors including hardware problems may present the same symptoms. TIP: Some websites have embedded miners that can mine cryptocurrency while you visit the page. While most browsers will block this, it may be something to investigate if you are experiencing an overheating computer while visiting certain websites.
I received a phone call that my PC reported a problem and this call centre person has been assigned to fix it. What should I do?	The WSJ website says about 350 million computers are sold each year. Imagine if only 10% give problems in one day - that means some "call centre" would need to make 35 million calls per day. As you can see, it's just not possible. And computers are not reporting their problems to a call centre to call you. What is happening is that this is a form of phishing combined with installation of Malware and sometimes Ransomware. DO NOT let anyone remotely control your computer

	to fix anything, especially if they called you. You should always be the one making the call for support to a number you know and trust.
My bank phoned me and said there is a problem with my banking application on my phone/ tablet - what should I do?	Your bank is not there to support you unless YOU called them. They do not originate calls through some kind of problem message from your phone. This is most probably a phishing call whereby they will ask you to go to a suspect web-site and enter your banking details or request them on the phone. Additionally, they may request your ATM or Credit-Card Temporary Transaction PIN/OTP. Never give these out.
I think my mobile phone has been hacked?	There are various things that could go wrong with a mobile phone or tablet. The following could be signs of a security concern on your device; Your device browser randomly opens to websites you did not browse to. People in your address book receive emails, or WhatsApp's or other messaging application messages that you did not send. Your battery life is extremely short, and you are not running any background applications such as navigation apps. Your data usage is very high, and you do not use any data-intensive applications.

Your Children & Teenagers

ISSUE / PROBLEM / TOPIC	RESOLUTION / ACTION
I think my Teenager/Child is becoming a Hacker!	Would you be this worried if the comment was "I think my child is becoming a lawyer?" Or "I think my child is becoming an Astro Physicist?" - either of those skills if abused could be used to do something bad. As I have mentioned elsewhere in this book, a hacker does not necessarily infer someone who is up to criminal activity or trying to sell weapons to another country. Your child could simply be interested in how things work - that is the core of what makes a hacker. A built-in need to see what things do when they're not used the way they're meant to be. Don't discourage a child from learning computer languages, reading about security and vulnerabilities or researching how things work. However, some signs may be something to look out for and - without panicking - discuss this issue with your child; A sudden hate-for or comments about another country or government that the child should not be concerned with at their age. This may indicate someone is trying to recruit them online. A sudden surge in money or financial gain without any indication of how such funds were received. Visits from persons you do not know, and a general lack of interest in explaining

how they know such persons.

Proceed with caution, so that you don't cause your child to lose trust in you as this will only complicate matters.

Your Banking & Finances

ISSUE / PROBLEM / TOPIC	RESOLUTION / ACTION
My Bank phoned to say my account has been compromised and they need my (Credit/Debit/ATM) Card PIN OR They need the One-Time-Pin sent to my Phone or Banking App OR They need me to approve an amount being charged on my Banking App in order to reverse it.	Your Bank controls all your finances. They do not need you to approve transactions in order to reverse them. It is thus very possible you are being Vished (Phishing via Voice Call). Never divulge PINs, Passwords or One-Time Passwords to someone over the phone. If in doubt, hang up the call and phone the bank yourself using their publicly available phone numbers to verify what has been said.
Someone brushed past me and I think they cloned my Contactless Bank Card	We brush up against people all the time, it does not mean they were all carrying devices to scan your contactless bank card. Unless you specifically saw a device, or someone actually aiming for your pocket or purse with a device, there is probably no need to worry. Further, you can fall back on the other security features of your card such as limits, in case someone did scan your card and cloned it. Check your transactions history for any suspicious payments and contact your Bank.
My Credit-Card was used online for purchases, but I never made those purchases.	This means your card data has been obtained somehow, through a hacked website, data leaks or cloned at a store. IF you have an additional security feature such as Verified-by-Visa or 3DSe-

cure by MasterCard, those should have protected you. If the Merchant selling goods bypassed them - they have taken all the risk and will be responsible for the loss when your bank reverses the transactions.

Either way, call your bank and report the fraud and request the transactions to be reversed and credited to your account.

Video Conferencing, Webinars and Other Webcam Usage

ISSUE / PROBLEM / TOPIC	RESOLUTION / ACTION
How do I ensure my on-line meetings are secure?	When it comes to online meetings using a webcam and microphone, you will always be at the mercy of the infrastructure used to facilitate the call or conference. That said, there is a lot being done to secure online communications. All the major conferencing software platforms such as Zoom, Microsoft Teams, Skype and so forth take active and ongoing precautions to secure their platforms. Some tips to keep in mind include; If you are able to, set a strong password for anyone to join a meeting. Use the "lobby" or "waiting" feature of the program that forces users to wait to be let into a meeting by the Host. This way you can screen who is actually trying to join. Don't broadcast meeting details openly. If you are planning a public event via video conference or webinar, remember that anyone can thus join. Disable the ability for non-Host users to share their screens or send media. Additionally, it may be a good idea to prevent chatting from people within the meeting unless required. If you don't need public participants, set the meeting to only allow those who are signed-in to the application with a

	valid account, and were invited, to join the meeting.
Should I have a cover on my webcam?	There are many stories that do the rounds about how attackers or governments were able to spy on people through their webcam. It is true, that some exploits can allow one to access a webcam. However, it would require a means of exploiting vulnerable software on your computer, not just a quick drive-by in a black van outside your home. The best answer to this is to do what makes you feel more comfortable. If you are worried someone could see you through your webcam, then activate the manual cover or put something over the camera.

IOT Devices & IOT Children's Toys

ISSUE / PROBLEM / TOPIC	RESOLUTION / ACTION
I bought my child an Internet of Things (IOT) Toy that connects to Wi-Fi. Should I be concerned?	"Connected" toys are all the rage these days with the interesting and sometimes useful functionality they provide. However, as discussed in Chapter 10, there are some things you need to be aware of: -Many, if not all, of these devices store their information on the cloud. You do not know where that data is stored, who has access to it nor how it is protected. - Devices with a microphone or camera could be sending photos, videos and audio files of your children and home to unknown locations and servers whose security is questionable. - Often, the access control is not built properly for these devices which could allow attackers to login and view, listen, or control the devices. It should be noted that many devices have increased their security posture and protection of data. However always be aware what you are allowing into your home.

Something strange happened to an IOT Device I own – I think it was hacked!	There are many things that could go wrong with an IOT device. Signs that someone else could have hacked the device are:
	    -The device performs actions on its own (such as a camera panning or turning without you being connected to it).
	    -The device plays sounds, or voices that are not you.

	-The device no longer lets you access it after performing one of the above.
	Whether or not the above occurs, if you are suspicious that your IOT device has been backed you should do two things: 1. Unplug the device and/or disconnect it from the network. 2. Reset the device back to factory settings and set it up again. If the problem persists, contact the device vendor. Also, ensure if you can set device passwords that they are set securely.
Which IOT devices are the safest to buy?	Unfortunately, I cannot answer this question for you. At least not by specifying which brands of devices are better than others. However, generally a device that has sold a lot has had a lot of focus on it and people have probably tried to find vulnerabilities in it. This is a good thing since highlighted vulnerabilities have hopefully been patched by the manufacturer. Do research on the Internet at reputable websites and then conclude for yourself whether the device is a secure buy or not. Also remember to follow the instructions on how to properly setup the device.